NUGGETS

100 BITES OF DAILY WISDOM

THOMAS C. BATTLE III

NUGGETS (100 BITES OF DAILY WISDOM)

ISBN: 978-1-7397009-9-7

Published by:
Grace House Publishing Company
www.gracehousepublishing.org

A book of inspirational quotes that will encourage you and push you to greater depths and higher heights.

"NEVER BE AFRAID TO LIVE ON PURPOSE WITH A PURPOSE FOR A PURPOSE."

~THOMAS C. BATTLE III~

CONTENTS

FOREWORD

In this book of quotes, readers will find inspiration, motivation, and wisdom from the author, Thomas C. Battle III, a dear friend of mine. From one who is a modern-day thinker, each quote has a unique perspective and relevance that can be applied to our daily lives.

But this book is not just a collection of random quotes. The carefully curated selection and thoughtful arrangement of the quotes lead to a profound realization that we are all connected in one way or another. Whether it's the pursuit of happiness, the quest for knowledge, the search for purpose or inner peace, or building stronger relationships, the universal themes of human existence are present in these quotes.

Thomas did a solid job on this one and I'm pretty sure as with his subsequent books. As you read through these pages, I trust that you will find meaning and purpose in each quote. They will inspire you to be the best version of yourself and to live the life you were meant to live. So, let us embark on this journey of self-discovery together, one quote at a time.

Way to go my friend. Bravo!

Femi Adun
Author/Global Speaker
Faith & Leadership Church, Scottsdale AZ

INTRODUCTION

> "TRUST IN THE LORD WITH ALL YOUR HEART,
> AND LEAN NOT TO YOUR OWN UNDERSTANDING; IN ALL YOUR WAYS
> ACKNOWLEDGE HIM, AND HE WILL DIRECT YOUR PATHS.
> PROVERBS 3:5-6"

Whenever we go through trials and tribulations in life, we always seem to run to a friend or family member, or we will find something so wrong to the point of calling our doctors and or our therapists.

But have you ever considered falling to your knees and asking God to help you in your walk with Him? Have you ever thought about just sitting down and taking a deep breath before you run to call on anyone?

Well, today is your day to rethink how you respond and react to life's challenges. It really doesn't matter how bad the situation is.
The question is, are you willing to rethink some decisions you have made in life to be a better you?

Many goals you struggle to accomplish in life can possibly be because of self-hate or maybe stagnating, but once you have completed this inspirational book of quotes, you will be well on your way to a better you and you will begin to have a clear understanding of what it means to be more than a conqueror!

~Battle~

POWER OF REPETITION

QUOTE #1

> "WHATEVER IT IS YOU CONSTANTLY ALLOW, WILL ALWAYS RESULT IN REPEATED FAILURES AND A LACK OF BETTER RESULTS."

~THOMAS C. BATTLE III~

THE FORCE OF CHARACTER

QUOTE #2

"IT IS NOT OUR ACHIEVEMENTS THAT SHOW WHO WE REALLY ARE. IT IS OUR CHARACTER."

~THOMAS C. BATTLE III~

THE PURSUIT OF PURPOSE

QUOTE #3

"ONCE YOU BEGIN TO PURSUE YOUR PURPOSE AND WHAT IT IS GOD HAS FOR YOU, IT WILL ALWAYS PRODUCE THE RIGHT BLESSINGS, AT THE RIGHT TIME, WITH THE RIGHT PEOPLE."

~THOMAS C. BATTLE III~

LIVING WITHOUT FEAR

QUOTE #4

> “ONCE YOU BEGIN TO LIVE
> WITHOUT FEAR,
> IT MAKES IT EASIER TO
> TRUST GOD.”

~THOMAS C. BATTLE III~

POWER OF FAITH

QUOTE #5

> “IT TAKES FAITH TO BE ABLE TO FOLLOW AND TRUST GOD.”

~THOMAS C. BATTLE III~

RULE OF PARTNERSHIP

QUOTE #6

> “KEEPING A PARTNERSHIP RELEVANT, REQUIRES YOU TO REPLENISH AND FULFILL THEIR NEEDS.”

~THOMAS C. BATTLE III~

THE LAW OF INFLUENCE

QUOTE #7

~THOMAS C. BATTLE III~

NO LIMIT MENTALITY

QUOTE #8

"I AM BRAVE BECAUSE I WAS CREATED TO LIVE BEYOND MY FEARS."

~THOMAS C. BATTLE III~

DITCHING YOUR FEARS

QUOTE #9

“AS YOU BEGIN TO LIVE YOUR LIFE BASED ON FAITH AND FAITH ALONE, NEVER LET FEAR FOLLOW.”

~THOMAS C. BATTLE III~

THE POWER OF READINESS

QUOTE #10

"MAKE SURE YOU STAY
RIGHT
AND STAY RIPE."

~THOMAS C. BATTLE III~

THE PRICE OF LEADING

QUOTE #11

> “LEADERSHIP REQUIRES YOU TO WEAR ARMOR TO PROTECT AND AN APRON TO SERVE.”

~THOMAS C. BATTLE III~

THE POWER OF LOVE

QUOTE #12

"ONCE YOU ACQUIRE AND UNDERSTAND REAL LOVE, IT MAKES IT EASIER TO OVERCOME EVIL."

~THOMAS C. BATTLE III~

THE POWER OF POSSIBILITIES

QUOTE #13

"NOTHING IN LIFE IS IMPOSSIBLE ONLY BECAUSE IT IS POSSIBLE TO CONQUER ALL THINGS WITH GOD ON YOUR SIDE."

~THOMAS C. BATTLE III~

UNIQUENESS AND SELF-MASTERY

QUOTE #14

“WE ALL LIVE IN THE SAME WORLD ON THE SAME PLANET, BUT WE ALL HAVE DIFFERENT PURPOSES, GIFTS, AND TALENTS TO ATTAIN.”

~THOMAS C. BATTLE III~

TRUE RELATIONSHIPS MATTER

QUOTE #15

“STANDARDS IN DIVINE AND REAL RELATIONSHIPS WILL ALWAYS ESTABLISH RESPECT AND BALANCE.”

~THOMAS C. BATTLE III~

NEEDS OVER WANTS

QUOTE #16

"NOWADAYS, PEOPLE WILL OVERVALUE THINGS THEY WANT, AND UNDERVALUE THE THINGS THEY NEED."

~THOMAS C. BATTLE III~

THE STRENGTH OF THE MIND

QUOTE #17

“A MIND THAT STAYS RENEWED AND REVIVED HAS THE POTENTIAL TO CREATE TRUE HAPPINESS IN THE HEART.”

~THOMAS C. BATTLE III~

THE PRICE OF LOVE

QUOTE #18

"LOVE WITHOUT
EVOLUTION IS AN
IRRELEVANT ACTION."

~THOMAS C. BATTLE III~

THE CHOICE IS YOURS

QUOTE #19

"EACH DAY OF YOUR LIFE CAN BE YOUR NEW BEGINNING OR THE FINAL STORY TO A CHAPTER IN YOUR BOOK."

~THOMAS C. BATTLE III~

THE IMPORTANCE OF GRATITUDE

QUOTE #20

"ALWAYS REMEMBER TO GIVE THANKS FOR THE THINGS GOD HAS DONE."

~THOMAS C. BATTLE III~

THE TEST OF LEADERSHIP

QUOTE #21

“WHEN YOU DESIRE TO LEAD, IT WILL ALWAYS REQUIRE YOU TO FOLLOW.”

~THOMAS C. BATTLE III~

THE LAW OF REFLECTION

QUOTE #22

"NEVER MISS OUT ON THE LESSONS YOU SHOULD LEARN WHEN YOU LOSE IN LIFE. IT WILL GET BETTER ONCE YOU APPLY THOSE LESSONS TO YOUR EVERYDAY LIVING."

~THOMAS C. BATTLE III~

DON'T GET IT TWISTED

QUOTE #23

“

THERE’S A DIFFERENCE BETWEEN A RINSE AND A CLEAN.
YOU WILL GET FURTHER IN LIFE ONCE YOU REALIZE AND RECOGNIZE THE DIFFERENCE.

”

~THOMAS C. BATTLE III~

THE STRENGTH OF IDENTITY

QUOTE #24

"THERE WOULDN'T BE A WOMAN IF IT WASN'T FOR A MAN."

~THOMAS C. BATTLE III~

DON'T BE A BULLY

QUOTE #25

"BEING INDEPENDENT DOES NOT GIVE YOU CONTROL OVER THE ONES THAT DEPEND ON YOU."

~THOMAS C. BATTLE III~

LEADERSHIP BY EXAMPLE

QUOTE #26

“LET YOUR LIFE INSPIRE
OTHERS TO LIVE.
BE THE CHANGE.”

~THOMAS C. BATTLE III~

FIRST WITH-IN
THEN
WITH-OUT

QUOTE #27

“IF YOU STRUGGLE WITH TRUE HAPPINESS WITHIN YOURSELF THEN YOU WILL NEVER DISCOVER TRUE HAPPINESS WITH OR IN ANYONE ELSE.”

~THOMAS C. BATTLE III~

LOVE IS BLIND

QUOTE #28

“HOMOSEXUALITY IS AN ARTIFICIAL LIFESTYLE THAT NEEDS REAL UNCONDITIONAL LOVE EFFECTIVELY.”

~THOMAS C. BATTLE III~

THE POWER OF VISION

QUOTE #29

"WHEN YOU DREAM WITH YOUR EYES OPEN, IT ALLOWS YOU TO ELIMINATE UNWANTED AND UNFULFILLING DESIRES FROM YOUR VISION."

~THOMAS C. BATTLE III~

UNDERSTANDING TRUE SUCCESS

QUOTE #30

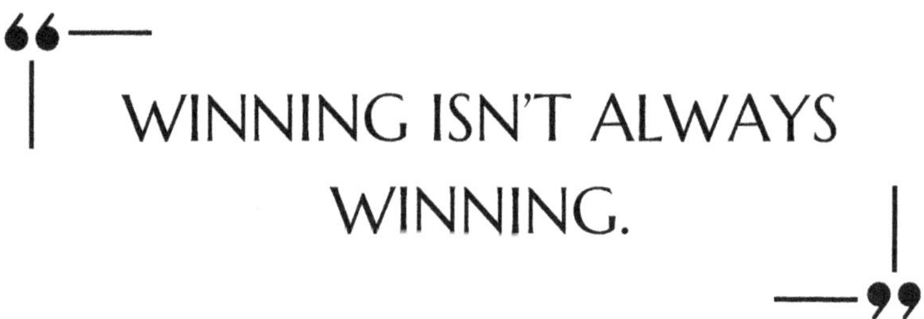

~THOMAS C. BATTLE III~

FINDING INNER PEACE

QUOTE #31

"IT IS IMPOSSIBLE TO GET AHEAD IN LIFE AND IN YOUR CAREER WHEN YOU ARE UNHAPPY WITH OTHERS AS WELL AS YOURSELF."

~THOMAS C. BATTLE III~

THE CALL IS YOURS

QUOTE #32

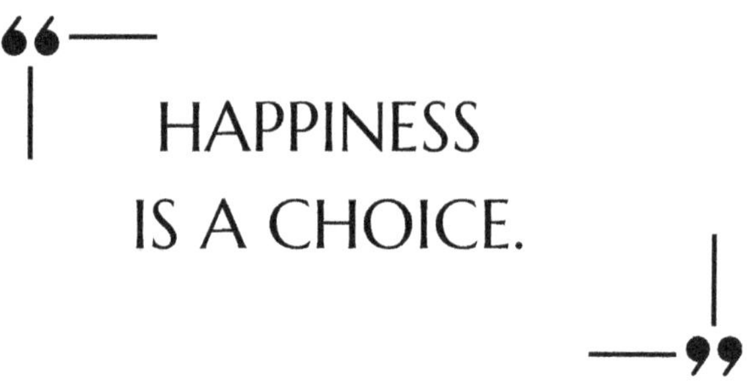

~THOMAS C. BATTLE III~

YOUR EMOTIONAL INTELIGENCE

QUOTE #33

"ONCE YOU REALIZE WHAT TRUE LOVE IS, YOU WILL NOT TRY TO LOVE OVER ANYTHING QUICKLY, BUT RATHER ENDURE IT AND SUSTAIN IT."

~THOMAS C. BATTLE III~

THE RELATIONSHIP MATRIX

QUOTE #34

"WOMEN SEEK SECURITY AND AFFECTION, WHILE MEN DESIRE RESPECT AND AUTHORITY."

~THOMAS C. BATTLE III~

THE POWER OF ASSOCIATION

QUOTE #35

"YOU CAN'T KEEP SHARKS AND TADPOLES IN THE SAME FISH TANK."

~THOMAS C. BATTLE III~

GOD
VS.
MAN

QUOTE #36

"MIRACLES ONLY COME FROM GOD. CONFUSION COMES FROM MAN."

~THOMAS C. BATTLE III~

THE STRENGTH OF SYNERGY

QUOTE #37

“THERE’S NO UNITY WITHOUT CONTINUED FAITH.”

~THOMAS C. BATTLE III~

THE LAW OF DISCERNMENT

QUOTE #38

"EITHER THEY ARE YOUR #1 ENEMY OR THEY ARE YOUR #1 HERO.
YOU MUST KNOW THE DIFFERENCE."

~THOMAS C. BATTLE III~

THE UNVEILING OF MASK

QUOTE #39

"A LOT OF PEOPLE YOU THOUGHT WERE FOR YOU ARE GOING TO EXPOSE THEMSELVES TO YOU WHO THEY REALLY ARE."

~THOMAS C. BATTLE III~

THIS FIGHT IS NOT YOURS

QUOTE #40

"IF IT IS NOT IN THEIR HEART TO CHANGE THEN THEY WON'T CHANGE. IT STARTS IN THE MIND, THE BODY, AND THEN YOUR SOUL."

~THOMAS C. BATTLE III~

TRUE STRENGTH OF A MAN

QUOTE #41

"A WISE MAN'S RESPONSE IS BETTER THAN A FOOLISH MAN'S REACTION."

~THOMAS C. BATTLE III~

KNOW WHERE TO INVEST

QUOTE #42

“NEVER LOSE YOURSELF TO OR FOR SOMEONE THAT IS NOT COMMITTED TO LOVING YOU WHOLE HEARTEDLY.”

~THOMAS C. BATTLE III~

STOP PLAYING AROUND

QUOTE #43

LIFE ISN'T ABOUT A GAME.
IT'S ABOUT GAIN.

~THOMAS C. BATTLE III~

STAY THE COURSE

QUOTE #44

“MARRIAGE IS NOT A UNIFORM.
YOU JUST CAN’T PUT IT ON AND TAKE IT OFF WHEN YOU FEEL LIKE IT.”

~THOMAS C. BATTLE III~

KEEP IT CLEAN

QUOTE #45

“INTIMACY IS A FORM OF COMMUNICATION. NEVER ABUSE IT.”

~THOMAS C. BATTLE III~

KEEP YOUR RHYTHM

QUOTE #46

“PEACE AND TRANQUILITY ARE NECESSARY WHEN YOU EXPERIENCE VARIOUS MOMENTS OF DEPRESSION AND ANXIETY.”

~THOMAS C. BATTLE III~

DON'T BE THE FOOL

QUOTE #47

"THE QUIETEST MAN IN THE ROOM CAN POSSIBLY BE THE MOST DANGEROUS MAN IN THE ROOM."

~THOMAS C. BATTLE III~

THE COST OF LASTING RELATIONSHIPS

QUOTE #48

"THE REAL TLC NEEDED IN ALL RELATIONSHIPS IS TRUST, LOYALTY, AND CONSISTENCY."

~THOMAS C. BATTLE III~

REWARDS AND DEMANDS

QUOTE #49

"ALTHOUGH THE ANOINTING AND CALLING ON YOUR LIFE CAN BE EXTREMELY ATTRACTIVE, IT COMES WITH MAJOR RESPONSIBILITIES AND GOD-GIVEN REWARDS."

~THOMAS C. BATTLE III~

PEACE AND BLESSING

QUOTE #50

"JESUS WAS GIVEN SO THAT
WE MAY FORGIVE.
IT'S A CHOICE BUT THE
BLESSINGS WILL FLOW
SMOOTHLY ONCE YOU
MAKE THIS A PART OF
YOUR EVERYDAY LIVING."

~THOMAS C. BATTLE III~

THE GENEROSITY LADDER

QUOTE #51

"GIVING IS THE MOST POWERFUL ACTION FROM ONE HUMAN BEING TO ANOTHER ON THIS PLANET.

~THOMAS C. BATTLE III~

STOP THE PROCASTINATION

QUOTE #52

"GIVE. GAVE. GOING TO.
ALWAYS TAKE ACTION."

~THOMAS C. BATTLE III~

DON'T EXPECT THE SAME FROM ALL

QUOTE #53

"SOME WILL CLIMB THE LADDER WITH YOU WHILE OTHERS WON'T EVEN CARRY THE LADDER FOR YOU."

~THOMAS C. BATTLE III~

BENEFITING FROM PRAYER

QUOTE #54

"A VERY ACCURATE PRAYER LIFE IS LIKE A COMPASS IN SOME OF THE MOST DIFFICULT TIMES.
IT GIVES YOU SPECIFIC DIRECTIONS AND GREAT DISCERNMENT."

~THOMAS C. BATTLE III~

IT IS NOT ONE-SIDED

QUOTE #55

“IF LOVE ISN'T RECIPROCATED, IT WILL ALWAYS LEAD TO HEARTBREAK AND FRUSTRATED MATES OR SPOUSES.
BE EQUAL OR CLOSE TO IT!”

~THOMAS C. BATTLE III~

TWO INGREDIENTS FOR SUCCESS

QUOTE #56

"WITH IMMENSE ACCOUNTABILITY AND MASSIVE CREATIVITY, YOUR INDIVIDUAL AND TEAMWORK WILL ALWAYS BE SUCCESSFUL."

~THOMAS C. BATTLE III~

THE BINDING FACTOR OF YOU TWO

QUOTE #57

"MARRIAGE IS SUPPOSED TO BE THE LIVING PRACTICE ACT OF FAITH."

~THOMAS C. BATTLE III~

IT IS NOT AN OPTION

QUOTE #58

"WHENEVER ONE BECOMES FRUSTRATED, ALWAYS TRY TO FIND A WAY TO BECOME FRUITFUL. YOU SOMETIMES WORK BEST WHEN YOU'RE UP AGAINST YOUR WORST. YOU GOT THIS!"

~THOMAS C. BATTLE III~

THE LOVE THAT NEVER FAILS

QUOTE #59

"UNCONDITIONAL LOVE IS NOT CREATED BY HUMAN BEINGS; IT IS CARRIED FOR HUMAN BEINGS."

~THOMAS C. BATTLE III~

THE INEVITABLE TEST

QUOTE #60

"IF YOU REALLY WANT TO SEE SOMEONE'S TRUE CHARACTER, WAIT TILL THEY FACE CHALLENGING TIMES."

~THOMAS C. BATTLE III~

IT'S NOT OVER WITH HIM

QUOTE #61

"GOD CAN AND WILL ALWAYS BE A GOD OF SECOND CHANCES IF YOU KEEP HIM FIRST IN YOUR LIFE."

~THOMAS C. BATTLE III~

THE LAW OF INTEGRITY

QUOTE #62

“PEOPLE WITH INTEGRITY WILL CONSTANTLY SEEK TO MAKE INTELLIGENT DECISIONS.”

~THOMAS C. BATTLE III~

THE COST OF ELEVATION

QUOTE #63

"ELEVATION CAUSES
TURBULENCE.
BE PREPARED FOR CHANGE.

~THOMAS C. BATTLE III~

THE LAW OF VISION

QUOTE #64

~THOMAS C. BATTLE III~

THE WILLINGNESS TO PAY

QUOTE #65

"THE PRICE OF LOVE IS THE COST OF ETERNAL LIFE, AS SHOWN BY JESUS CHRIST. WHAT WILL BE YOUR SACRIFICE?"

~THOMAS C. BATTLE III~

DEPLOY YOUR FAITH

QUOTE #66

"THERE'S NO PRICE TAG ON
FAITH.
YOU MUST APPLY IT TO
YOUR EVERYDAY LIVING
AND ALWAYS TRUST THAT
GOD WILL SEE YOU
THROUGH.
THAT IS PRICELESS."

~THOMAS C. BATTLE III~

DON'T SIT ON YOUR DREAMS

QUOTE #67

"ONCE YOU CAN FOLLOW YOUR DREAMS, THEY WILL MORE THAN LIKELY LEAD YOU TO YOUR DESTINY."

~THOMAS C. BATTLE III~

THE CODE FOR A FRESH START

QUOTE #68

"GOD'S GIFT OF FORGIVENESS TO US ALL IS KEY TO A FRESH START FOR NEW OPPORTUNITIES, GRACE, AND FAVOR."

~THOMAS C. BATTLE III~

DON'T GET CAUGHT UP

QUOTE #69

“NEVER BE AFRAID TO EXCEED THOSE EXPECTATIONS OF YOU FROM OTHERS. MOST DON’T WANT TO SEE YOU MAKE IT.
BE GREAT ANYWAY.”

~THOMAS C. BATTLE III~

JUST ONE MOVE

QUOTE #70

"THE SECRET TO GETTING AHEAD IS GETTING BEYOND THE STARTING POINT. YOU HAVE TO START"

~THOMAS C. BATTLE III~

ALWAYS SEE THE GOOD

QUOTE #71

"HAVE FAITH IN THE POTENTIAL OF THE BELIEVING."

~THOMAS C. BATTLE III~

CHOOSE THE WISELY

QUOTE #72

"EVERY SINGLE DAY OF YOUR LIFE WILL HAVE THE OPPORTUNITY TO CHALLENGE AND OR CHANGE YOU."

~THOMAS C. BATTLE III~

HANDLE YOUR BUSINESS

QUOTE #73

"YOU CAN ONLY LIMIT YOURSELF.
SO WHY LET OTHERS DO IT AS WELL?"

~THOMAS C. BATTLE III~

HOW DO YOU SEE IT

QUOTE #74

“MOST OBSTACLES IN YOUR LIFE ARE DESIGNED TO HELP YOU CLIMB UP AND OUT OF YOUR SITUATIONS
SO YOU CAN GROW AND ESTABLISH STABILITY FOR THE GREATER GOOD.”

~THOMAS C. BATTLE III~

A
NEW
WAY

QUOTE #75

"IF YOU DESIRE SOMETHING
YOU'VE NEVER HAD, THEN
YOU MUST BE MORE
THAN WILLING TO
DO SOME THINGS
YOU'VE NEVER DONE"

~THOMAS C. BATTLE III~

SWITCH THE PERSPECTIVE

QUOTE #76

“MISTAKES ARE
EVIDENCE THAT YOU’VE
BEEN TRYING.”

~THOMAS C. BATTLE III~

MIND THE GAP

QUOTE #77

"THERE'S NOTHING AVERAGE ABOUT AN ACHIEVER'S MENTALITY."

~THOMAS C. BATTLE III~

BIGGER AND BETTER

QUOTE #78

"NEVER DOWNSIZE YOUR GREATNESS BY CONTINUOUSLY CHOOSING TO STAY INSIDE YOUR COMFORT ZONE."

~THOMAS C. BATTLE III~

WALK THE TALK

QUOTE #79

“A WORD THAT IS
READ AND PUTTING INTO
ACTION IS WHAT
CAUSES A REACTION.”

~THOMAS C. BATTLE III~

DO IT NOW

QUOTE #80

LET IT GO.

~THOMAS C. BATTLE III~

A RULE OF LIVE

QUOTE #81

~THOMAS C. BATTLE III~

WHAT DO YOU BELIEVE

QUOTE #82

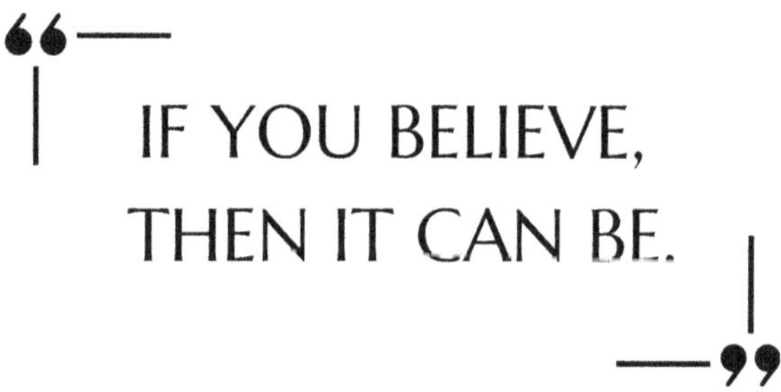

~THOMAS C. BATTLE III~

GO
GET
IT

QUOTE #83

"YOU CANNOT LOSE
SOMETHING YOU NEVER
HAD.
PRAY FOR WHAT YOU WANT
AND BELIEVE YOU WILL
RECEIVE."

~THOMAS C. BATTLE III~

A TRUE PLAYER

QUOTE #84

> IT TAKES MATURITY AND WISDOM TO MAKE PEACE WITH FOOLISH PEOPLE.

~THOMAS C. BATTLE III~

THE PURPOSE CODE

QUOTE #85

“NEVER BE AFRAID TO
LIVE ON PURPOSE WITH
A PURPOSE
FOR A PURPOSE.”

~THOMAS C. BATTLE III~

HOW IT ALL ENDS

QUOTE #86

"EVERY TRIAL AND TRIBULATION YOU OVERCOME BRINGS YOU A STEP CLOSER TO BETTER AND ENDLESS OPPORTUNITIES IN LIFE."

~THOMAS C. BATTLE III~

NO RETREAT, NO SURRENDER

QUOTE #87

"NEVER GIVE UP AMID YOUR TROUBLES FOR IT IS THEN, YOUR TROUBLES WILL STRENGTHEN YOUR FOUNDATION."

~THOMAS C. BATTLE III~

BEYOND THE IMAGINATION

QUOTE #88

GOD CAN BLESS YOU IN WAYS THAT WILL HAVE OTHERS QUESTIONING, "HOW?"

~THOMAS C. BATTLE III~

THE FAMILY CODE

QUOTE #89

“RAISING A FAMILY AND WORKING HARD WILL TEACH YOU PATIENCE AND UNCONDITIONAL LOVE.”

~THOMAS C. BATTLE III~

HIM FIRST AND THEM

QUOTE #90

"YOU MUST FIRST
LEAN
ON YOUR FAITH
IN GOD AND LOVE
MORE ON YOUR FAMILY."

~THOMAS C. BATTLE III~

UNCOVERING YOUR AUTHENTIC SELF

QUOTE #91

"YOUR CHALLENGES
IN LIFE WILL REVEAL YOUR
MEASURE OF FAITH JUST LIKE
ACCOUNTABILITY WILL
REVEAL YOUR CHARACTER."

~THOMAS C. BATTLE III~

GOD IN THE MIX

QUOTE #92

"TRUST GOD'S WORD AND HAVE COMMON SENSE."

~THOMAS C. BATTLE III~

SURVIVAL OF THE FITTEST

QUOTE #93

"ONLY THE STRONG SURVIVE WHEN THEY HAVE COME TO GRIPS WITH LIFE WITHOUT LETTING GO."

~THOMAS C. BATTLE III~

MAKE YOUR BUSINESS A BUSINESS

QUOTE #94

“LIFE CAN BE DIFFICULT, OR IT CAN BE AT PEACE IF YOU KNOW HOW TO HANDLE YOUR SITUATIONS PROPERLY.”

~THOMAS C. BATTLE III~

COOL
CALM
COLLECTED

QUOTE #95

NEVER LET YOUR HATERS SEE YOU SWEAT. THEY THRIVE OFF YOUR WEAKNESS.

~THOMAS C. BATTLE III~

PASS IT ONE

QUOTE #96

"IT IS SO AMAZING HOW SO
MANY PEOPLE CAN HATE
YOU THAT DON'T EVEN
KNOW YOU.
THEIR TROUBLES ARE NOT
YOURS!"

~THOMAS C. BATTLE III~

TIME TELLS IT BETTER

QUOTE #97

"WHEN IT'S TIME FOR IT ALL
TO MAKE SENSE,
IT WILL. DO NOT GIVE UP. DO
NOT GIVE IN."

~THOMAS C. BATTLE III~

PAST IN THE PAST

QUOTE #98

“NEVER GIVE UP ON YOUR DREAMS BECAUSE SOMEONE TOLD YOU THAT YOU WERE A FAILURE.
THERE’S A DIFFERENCE BETWEEN THEN AND NOW.”

~THOMAS C. BATTLE III~

ENJOY
YOUR
LIFE

QUOTE #99

“LIVE LIFE TO THE FULLEST
WITH NO REGRETS
AND NO HATE.”

~THOMAS C. BATTLE III~

GET TO THE FINISHING LINE

QUOTE #100

“YOU ARE A WINNER.
ALWAYS KEEP
GOD FIRST.”

~THOMAS C. BATTLE III~

NUGGETS

The purpose of writing this quote book was simply to capture my audience's attention and to strike hope in their hearts.

I pray this first book of quotes will cause you to rethink your lack of faith, love your family more, and never give up on God or in life.

People often will try to intimidate you and doubt you when you are pursuing your dreams because they do not have a sense of purpose.

Leave them behind and press toward the mark.
Your calling and reasoning for life are in front of you.
Not behind you!
Go forth!

~THOMAS C. BATTLE III~

MY APPRECIATION

Dear All,

I would like to extend my heartfelt gratitude to everyone who played a role in the publication of my book. It is a dream come true to see my work in the form of a physical book, and I am eternally grateful for the opportunity and support provided to me.

I would like to thank my publisher (Grace House Publishing) for believing in my work and for their efforts in making it available to readers across the world. To my friends, family, and colleagues, thank you for being my inspiration and for your encouragement towards my writing.

Lastly, I would like to thank my readers who have already begun to read my book. Your support and feedback mean everything to me, and I hope that my work can touch your lives in a meaningful way.

Thank you all for your unwavering support and encouragement. I am truly grateful to have you in my life.
Sincerely,

~THOMAS C. BATTLE III~

EMAIL
THOMAS C. BATTLE III
AT:
CHIEFBATTLE3@GMAIL.COM

Made in the USA
Monee, IL
03 July 2023

38015401R10116